Housework

Chris Clark and Bobbie Neate

This book is about the work we all do in our houses.

You do not have to read this book from beginning to end.
Just turn to the pages that interest you.

Contents

What is housework?

Housework can be many different jobs. We often talk about "doing the housework" when we are cleaning the home but there are other jobs as well.

Housework is washing and ironing and mending clothes.
Housework is tidying up, cleaning, dusting and sweeping.
It is also making the beds.
Housework is preparing meals, clearing the table and
washing up.

Sometimes there are jobs like looking after animals,
getting food and fetching water.

Why do we do housework?

We collect water to drink, to cook and to wash with.

We keep animals so that they can give us milk and meat to eat.

We feed the animals so that they will grow strong and healthy.

We dust, sweep and clean the home so it is pleasant to live in.

We prepare the food so that we can have good meals to eat.

We wash and iron clothes to keep them clean and smart.

What can we use for housework?

Here are some of the things we can use for housework.

↑ We can use cloths for dusting and cleaning.

↑ We can use brushes to sweep away the dust on the floor.

↑ We can use soap and detergents to make our clothes clean.

▲ We can use fires, ovens or cookers to cook food.

▲ We can use pots to carry the water in.

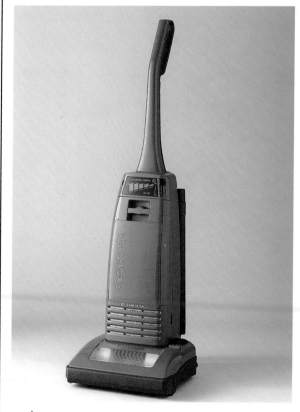

▲ There are some machines to help us with housework.

How do we do housework?

How to clean a room.

First you tidy the room and put things away.

Then you dust or wipe the shelves and surfaces.

Then you sweep the floor.

One way to collect water.

First you collect the pots to carry the water in.

Then you walk to the watering hole. Sometimes it is a very long walk.

You put the pot in the water and fill it up.

Then you can carry the pot home. It is often best to carry the pot on your head.

One way to wash clothes.

First you fill up a bowl with warm water.

Then you put in some soap powder.

Next you put the clothes in the water. You rub the clothes in the soapy water.

Then you fill up another bowl with clean water.

You rinse the clothes in this water to get the soap out.

Then you have to squeeze out the water.

Then you leave the clothes to dry.

Who does housework?

Everybody in the family can do housework.

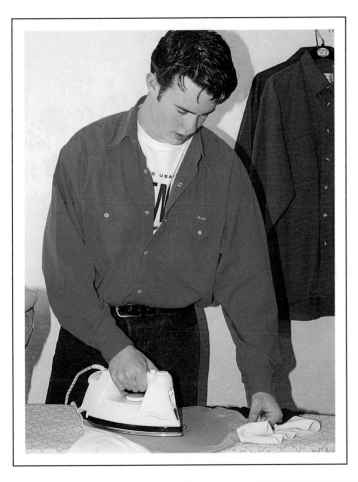

In some homes everybody helps with all the jobs but in other homes the jobs are done by just one member of the family.

	mum	dad	Peter	Susan	Robert
making bed		✓	✓	✓	✓
washing up	✓	✓	✓		
washing clothes	✓				
ironing		✓			
tidying up	✓	✓	✓	✓	✓
vacuuming floors	✓	✓	✓		
polishing furniture			✓	✓	✓
dusting				✓	✓
preparing meals	✓	✓			

Rich families in Britain one hundred years ago

Some rich families lived in very big houses.
The rich people did not do much housework.
They told their servants what to do.

⬆ Servants worked for 14 or 15 hours each day. They worked very hard.

The servants who worked in big houses
all had special jobs to do.
Some servants kept the house clean and tidy.
Some servants worked in the kitchens,
making food and cleaning up after meals.

Some servants had to clean and light the fire early in the morning.

Poor families in Britain one hundred years ago

One hundred years ago housework was very hard work for poor families. The women had to do many jobs. The jobs took them a long time.

⬆ There was no water in the home so washing and cleaning were difficult.

🔺 Mum's first job at five o'clock in the morning was to light the fire.

The mother had to prepare the meals without any machines to help her. It took a long time to make a meal. She had to wash all the clothes by hand and iron them. She always mended the clothes.

Housework in other countries

Mali

Mali is a country in Africa.
Some people in Mali do not have water or electricity in their homes but the hot weather in Mali makes drying the clothes easy.

⬆ Some rich families in Africa have many machines to help with the housework.

Some people have water and electricity in their homes and machines to help them with the housework.
They might also have someone to help them with the jobs.

Other people have many jobs to do and it takes them a long time to do the housework. Food is often prepared and cooked outside.

Food is often cooked over a fire. ➤➤

⬆ Sometimes women from Mali wash their clothes in the river.

China

In China the women and the children usually do the housework.

⬆ In China the women and children collect the water..

In many Chinese homes the washing is done by the mother and her daughters. They do the washing by hand. In some towns and villages there is no water in the houses.

18

In China cooking is done on a stove. It is often the children who collect the firewood for the stove.

⬆ The stove can burn a lot of firewood.

Inventions that help do housework

Housework is usually easier when there are machines to do the work.

Most machines need electricity to make them work. Vacuum cleaners, food mixers, washing machines and tumble driers all use electricity. Some people do not like machines to help them with the housework.

A vacuum cleaner sucks up dust and dirt.

An electric iron makes ironing quick and easy.

⬆ Automatic washing machines wash a lot of clothes.

⬆ Food mixers and processors stop your arm from aching.

Should we clear the table straight away?

Yes or No

The food can be used for another meal.

The plates are easier to clean because the food has not stuck to them.

The room looks tidy.

The table can be used for other things.

The food is stale, it has gone off.

The plates are very difficult to clean.

The room looks awful.

The table cannot be used.

Glossary of words used in this book

Aching　　　　　When you are aching your body hurts.

Automatic　　　An automatic washing machine is a machine that will wash,
washing machine　rinse and spin clothes.

Dusting　　　　Dusting is taking away the dust in a house. We do this with a duster.

Firewood　　　Firewood is small pieces of dry wood. They are used to light a fire.

Food processor　A food processor is a machine which cuts or chops food.

Soap powder　　Soap powder is like washing powder but it is made of
　　　　　　　　nothing but soap.

Squeeze　　　When you squeeze something you press it very tightly.

Stove　　　　A stove is a kind of cooker. It is also used for heating.

Vacuum cleaner　A vacuum cleaner is a machine that sucks up dirt.
　　　　　　　　Its motor is worked by electricity.

Index

a b c d e f g h i j k l m n o p q r s t u v w x y z
A B C D E F G H I J K L M N O P Q R S T U V W X Y Z